Feminist Criticisms:

A Look at Different Points of View

By

Nick Graham

Table Of Contents

Introduction

The rights, equality, and empowerment of women in all spheres of society are the goals of feminism, a multidimensional and dynamic sociopolitical and cultural movement. Feminism includes a wide variety of viewpoints, ideas, and methods, even though its primary objective is to address and correct gender-based injustices and inequities.

Fundamentals of Feminism

Gender Equality

Feminism's fundamental goal is to achieve gender equality. It questions and works to eliminate societal institutions, norms, and behaviors that uphold discrimination or disadvantage on the basis of gender.

Empowerment

Feminism promotes the agency, voice, and control of women and other marginalized people over their lives, decisions, and bodies. This empowerment includes aspects like personal liberty, work, and education.

Feminism frequently supports larger social justice initiatives. It acknowledges the connections between gender and other identification factors like race, class, sexual orientation, and disability. As a result, feminism usually aims to combat overlapping oppression and prejudice.

Diversity of Viewpoints
The feminist movement is not one-sided or consistent. It includes a diverse spectrum of viewpoints and theories. Liberal feminism (focusing on legal and political reforms), radical feminism (addressing larger societal structures), intersectional feminism (emphasizing the interaction of various identities),

and others are some common branches of feminism.

Historical Origins

The campaign for women's suffrage has historical origins that may be traced to the late 19th and early 20th centuries. Important turning points in this history include the suffrage movements. Feminism has changed and grown over time to accommodate shifting social conditions.

Activism

Feminism is frequently linked to many types of activism, such as protests, advocacy, public awareness campaigns, and grassroots organizing. Women's rights activists strive to bring about change on a local, national, and worldwide scale.

Feminism is constantly changing in response to societal changes and fresh problems. It continues to be an active, changing discourse that responds to the shifting demands and issues of women and other oppressed groups.

In various respects, constructive critique is essential for growing feminist discourse.

Self-Reflection and Growth

Feminists are urged to consider their attitudes, plans, and methods by constructive critique. It forces individuals to reflect on whether their choices are consistent with their values and objectives. Feminism can develop and adapt through this process to better answer the shifting demands and difficulties experienced by women and underprivileged groups.

Constructive criticism aids feminists in becoming aware of any biases or blind spots in their viewpoints. It may draw attention to instances in which particular viewpoints or problems have been disregarded or neglected within the movement. By ensuring that the issues of other groups are taken into account, this understanding encourages a more inclusive and intersectional approach to feminism.

Intellectual Engagement

In feminist circles, constructive criticism fosters discussion and intellectual engagement. It encourages discussion and the sharing of ideas, enabling feminists to hone their arguments, disprove presumptions, and gain a deeper comprehension of intricate problems relating to gender and injustice.

Building Alliances

Critique can help feminists from various views find areas of agreement and shared objectives. It can aid in bridging movement rifts and forging ties with people and groups that might have previously felt marginalized or alienated.

Innovation and Creativity

Within feminist discourse, criticism can encourage innovation and creativity. It may provide fresh perspectives, ideas, and answers to persistent gender-based issues. This innovative thinking can be helpful in bringing about change and accomplishing feminist objectives.

Constructive criticism can aid feminists in strengthening their resilience in the face of adversity or rejection from outside sources. Feminists can improve their ability to respond to external criticisms and opposition to measures for gender equality by addressing internal difficulties and criticisms.

Accountability

Feminists are held responsible for their deeds and attitudes by constructive criticism. It promotes honesty and moral conduct in the movement. Accountability is crucial for preserving credibility and confidence in the larger community as well as among feminist circles.

Balanced Advocacy

Feminists can strike a balance between promoting women's rights and taking into account the broader social repercussions of their actions by taking into account various viewpoints and potential downsides of particular techniques. A larger audience may find feminism more sympathetic and persuasive with this well-rounded approach.

Chapter 1

Gender-Based Diverseness

As a broad and multifaceted movement, feminism has influenced gender dynamics in many ways, and in some cases, it has been thought to be dividing people into different genders. It's crucial to remember that these consequences might be attributed to certain feminisms, behaviors, or interpretations of feminist ideology rather than being general or inherent to feminism as a whole. Feminism has been attacked in the following ways for possibly causing gender divisions:

Perceived Generalizations

According to some detractors, some feminist rhetoric and arguments generalize about men, depicting them as a singular group to blame for societal injustices. Men who do not identify with these preconceptions may feel resentful or alienated as a result of such judgments.

Negative Stereotyping

Feminist discourse has occasionally come under fire for promoting false notions about masculinity, depicting it as poisonous or harmful by nature. Given that it might not recognize the variety of masculine identities and experiences, this has the potential to be contentious.

Us vs. Them attitude

According to critics, some feminist viewpoints can foster an "us vs. them" attitude in which advances for women are seen as losses for males and gender issues are presented as a zero-sum game. This framing can obstruct gender-inclusive communication and collaboration.

Men as Bystanders

Inadvertently, certain feminist critiques of patriarchy and gender-based violence may portray men predominantly as perpetrators or bystanders. This viewpoint may undervalue the contribution of male allies and advocates for gender equality.

Resistance and Backlash

The idea that feminism is a divisive force has occasionally sparked opposition and backlash from some sections of society, especially men who could see feminism as a threat to their interests or identity. This opposition may exacerbate existing divisions.

The fact that feminism is not a homogenous movement and that different feminists have varied viewpoints on these issues must be emphasized. Numerous feminists actively promote gender equality and stress the value of intergender collaboration, communication, and solidarity. Feminism has also been crucial in pushing for changes that are advantageous to individuals of all genders, such as opposing conventional gender roles and encouraging healthy forms of masculinity.

The broader conversation on gender equality includes critiques and analyses of gender roles and feminism. They emphasize the significance of inclusive and nuanced feminist perspectives that respect the experiences and viewpoints of all people, regardless of gender, and aim to promote greater understanding and collaboration between sexes.

Chapter 2

Victimhood Culture

Some people, frequently as a criticism of specific elements of contemporary feminist rhetoric, assert that feminism encourages a "victimhood culture" among women. It's critical to remember that this criticism is based on particular interpretations of feminism and is not generally accepted. Following are several justifications and viewpoints for this criticism:

Overemphasis on Victimhood

Some feminist narratives and discourses, according to their detractors, place an excessive amount of emphasis on portraying women as the victims of patriarchal tyranny. They argue that this focus on victimhood can increase women's feelings of dependence and helplessness.

Dependence on External Solutions

According to some detractors, presenting women as victims can encourage people to think that government regulations or outside interventions are the main ways to address gender-based problems. This viewpoint might minimize the agency and ability of women to bring about change on their own.

Identity politics, when people primarily define themselves by their group identity (in this case, gender) and their perceived victimization, is said to be the result of a concentration on victimhood that is too great. This might obstruct the growth of a society that is more inclusive and cohesive.

Emphasizing Victimhood Can Perpetuate a Negative Narrative That Paints Women as Permanently Oppressed, Potentially Shadowing Progress Made in Addressing Gender-Based Inequalities, According to Critics.

Some critics contend that the victimhood narrative may limit women's perceptions of their own strength and efficacy. They contend that rather than concentrating simply on women's victimization, empowerment can be promoted by emphasizing women's talents, accomplishments, and capacity for change.

It's critical to understand that feminism is a broad and dynamic movement with many different points of view and that not all feminists or feminist discourse stress victimhood. Many feminisms promote agency, resilience, and empowerment, highlighting women's capacity to question social conventions and bring about good change. Additionally, criticisms like these frequently originate from a perspective that might not completely take into account the historical and current gender-based injustices that women have experienced.

The overall goal of feminism is to eliminate gender-based discrimination and advance gender equality. While criticisms like the one concerning a "victimhood culture" might spark crucial dialogues about how gender issues are framed and communicated, they only reflect one aspect of a larger and more complex movement. These topics may be approached by various feminists and feminist organizations in various and complex ways.

Chapter 3

Economic Consequences

Critics of certain feminist initiatives claim that while these policies are well-intentioned and aimed at resolving gender-based disparities, they can occasionally have unexpected economic implications. It's crucial to highlight that these critiques are presented in the context of specific policies and should not be interpreted as an overall rejection of gender equality aims. Here are some examples of how certain feminist measures may have unforeseen economic consequences:

Affirmative Action and Gender-Based Quotas

Affirmative action programs or gender-based quotas strive to boost the presence of women in certain areas or positions, such as corporate boards or political offices. Critics contend that these practices may accidentally lead to negative economic consequences:

Meritocracy Concerns

Critics claim that such regulations may stress gender above merit, potentially leading to persons being chosen for positions based on their gender rather than their qualifications. This, they suggest, could degrade the overall competency and effectiveness of organizations or institutions.

Backlash

Some critics claim that affirmative action and quotas might lead to a backlash among people who regard themselves as disadvantaged by these programs, potentially resulting in less cooperation or resistance.

Stigmatization

Critics believe that affirmative action might stigmatize women or minority groups, producing views that they are not capable of attaining success on their own merits.

Paid Parental Leave Policies

While paid parental leave policies are designed to benefit working parents, critics claim that they can have unexpected economic consequences:

Labor Market Effects

Some critics claim that generous paid parental leave laws may lead to companies being less eager to hire women of childbearing age, fearing the costs connected with maternity leave.

This could result in gender-based discrimination in hiring.

Reduced Earnings

Critics believe that long periods of parental leave might lead to reduced lifetime earnings for women if they spend a major amount of their career on leave or working part-time.

Economic expense on Employers

Critics say that the financial expense of providing paid maternity leave may disproportionately affect small enterprises, perhaps leading to job losses or diminished employment possibilities.

Equal Pay Initiatives

While initiatives to address the gender pay gap are universally accepted, detractors contend that certain measures can have unexpected consequences:

Regulatory Burden

Some critics claim that stringent restrictions intended at ensuring equal pay might create a regulatory burden for firms, either limiting job creation or leading to limited flexibility in salary negotiations.

Focus on Salary over advantages

Critics claim that measures oriented primarily at equalizing salaries may lead to employers offering fewer non-salary advantages, such as flexible work arrangements or bonuses, which can be particularly helpful to women.

It's crucial to understand that the unintended implications of legislation might differ depending on the specific environment, execution, and societal standards. Policymakers and supporters must carefully evaluate any unintended consequences when drafting and implementing gender equality legislation, trying to strike a balance that achieves gender equality while reducing negative economic implications. Additionally, these critiques should not obscure the broader aims of gender equality, which are vital to establishing a more equitable and inclusive society.

Chapter 4

Freedom of Choice

A concept within feminism known as "choice feminism" emphasizes the value of women's autonomy in determining the course of their lives, including decisions on their careers, families, intimate relationships, and personal expression. It acknowledges that women need to be allowed the freedom to make decisions that are consistent with their own values, wants, and circumstances, free from criticism or social pressures that would dictate what those decisions should be.

The following are significant choices for feminism's implications:

Empowerment and Autonomy

Options Women's autonomy and empowerment are highly valued by feminism. It states that women should have the freedom to make decisions that reflect their own circumstances and objectives since they are the best judges of their own lives.

Rejecting Prescriptive Norms

It opposes societal expectations and established gender norms that set forth particular responsibilities and actions for women. According to choice feminism, there is no one model that applies to all women's lives and they shouldn't be constrained by societal standards or prejudices.

Various Routes to Empowerment

Options Feminism acknowledges that empowerment can take many different forms and that one woman may not be empowered in the same way as another. This viewpoint values many ways of living, whether they involve focusing on a profession, a family, or taking unorthodox routes.

Respect for Individual Choices

It urges against passing judgment on women's decisions. Being a stay-at-home mom, pursuing a successful job, or adopting alternative lifestyles are all viable choices that should be supported under a choice feminist paradigm.

Cross-sectionality

Option Feminism and the idea of intersectionality interact because feminism acknowledges that characteristics like color, class, sexual orientation, and disability affect the options open to women. It highlights how crucial it is to examine many facets of privilege and identity when talking about choices.

Choice feminism questions the external influences and expectations that frequently specify how women should conduct their lives. It empowers women to defy stereotypes and societal standards and make decisions based on their own needs and wants.

Choice feminism's effects may include:

Greater Individual Freedom

Women have more control over their lives and more freedom to choose the pathways that truly reflect their values and objectives.

Reduced Gender-Based Limits

Choice feminism helps to lessen the limits and limitations imposed on women's choices by challenging traditional gender roles and expectations.

Promotion of inclusion

Choice feminism fosters inclusion by acknowledging that not all women have equal opportunities and that choices have to be recognized in the context of various circumstances and experiences.

It recognizes that not all women have the same amount of freedom to choose, and that attempts to empower women should take into account and address the overlapping forces of privilege and oppression.

Choice feminism can advance a more inclusive and equitable society where women are free to make decisions that lead to happy lives on their own terms, defying gender conventions in the process. This has a beneficial effect on gender equality.

It's critical to remember that choice feminism has its detractors, despite being liberating for many. Some claim that it might ignore the structural injustices and limitations on women's choices. Choice feminism's proponents stress that these efforts should be seen as a complement to larger feminist initiatives aiming at removing these obstacles and building a more inclusive and equal society for all women.

Chapter 5

Inclusivity and Marginalization

Some feminist movements have come under fire for allegedly excluding or undervaluing men in their words and deeds. It's critical to understand that these issues don't represent all feminist movements or viewpoints, and that many feminists actively seek out men to join them in the battle for gender equality. Here are some issues and criticisms regarding the marginalization or exclusion of males in some feminist situations, though:

Generalization and Stereotyping

Some feminist talks and language, according to critics, may generalize or stereotype men, depicting them as being solely to blame for gender-based injustices. Men who do not fit these preconceptions may have negative judgments and a sense of estrangement as a result.

Lack of Inclusivity

According to some detractors, some feminist gatherings or spaces may not be open to males, thereby keeping them out of crucial discussions about gender equality. Men may be deterred from actively supporting feminist initiatives by this lack of inclusivity.

Men have occasionally reported feeling uncomfortable or encountering hostility at feminist forums or discussions. Men may be discouraged from discussing gender issues or acting as allies as a result of this.

Focus on Women's Issues Only

According to detractors, some feminist movements could put more of an emphasis on women's issues than on those that affect males. While focusing on women's issues is important, it is ideal for this focus to coexist alongside an understanding of the particular difficulties and injustices that males may encounter.

Men's traditional masculinity has been criticized by some feminists, who have been accused of undermining or criticizing masculinity itself. Critics contend that addressing negative aspects of masculinity while recognizing positive manifestations of masculinity requires a more nuanced strategy.

Gender-Neutral vocabulary

To make sure that men and people of all genders feel included in debates on gender equality, some critics support the use of gender-neutral vocabulary in feminism.

Engaging males as Allies

According to detractors, greater action has to be taken to involve males in the feminist cause as allies. This involves encouraging males to get involved in campaigns, education, and advocacy for gender equality.

Intersectionality and Inclusive Feminism

Some detractors of feminism contend that taking an intersectional stance, which recognizes the interconnectedness of different facets of identity (such as race, class, sexual orientation, and gender), can result in a more inclusive feminist movement that takes into account the various life experiences of all people.

It's critical to emphasize that these criticisms represent particular viewpoints within a larger feminist landscape. In an effort to create a society that is more inclusive and equal, many feminists actively seek out males as allies. Additionally, efforts to address issues affecting males should not be considered incompatible with feminist concepts but rather as complimentary in the larger fight for gender justice because gender equality is a common objective that benefits individuals of all genders.

What part do males play in promoting gender equality?

Men must play a significant part in promoting gender equality. Gender equality is a social issue that calls for the active participation and support of individuals of all genders. It is not just a women's issue. Men can play the following important roles in furthering gender equality:

Men can actively support and push for equal opportunities for women in a variety of areas of life, such as leadership positions, the workforce, and education. This may entail backing laws and procedures intended to end discrimination based on gender.

Defeating preconceptions and Bias

Men can fight negative gender preconceptions and biases and dismantle them. This entails acknowledging and addressing one's own biases as well as promoting considerate and inclusive conduct in one's social and professional networks.

Men can become knowledgeable allies by educating themselves on gender-related topics. This entails being aware of the broader social and systemic issues that lead to gender inequality as well as the experiences and difficulties faced by women and other oppressed genders.

Men may actively listen to the viewpoints and experiences of women and other marginalized genders, amplifying their voices in the process. They can amplify these voices and make sure they are heard and valued by using their power and privilege.

Men can promote women's representation and leadership in a variety of professions, such as politics, business, academia, and the arts. This involves promoting gender-balanced leadership teams and serving as a mentor or sponsor.

Men can question traditional gender norms in childcare and parenting to support equal parenting. This entails actively taking on caregiving duties and supporting workplace policies and procedures that let men and women both manage work and family obligations.

Men may actively work to stop and confront gender-based violence, whether it occurs in their intimate relationships or the larger community. This entails helping survivors and stepping in when harmful behavior is observed.

Men can participate in advocacy activities to improve gender equality, such as sponsoring groups and projects that promote gender justice. They might also take part in activities and campaigns to raise public awareness about gender inequality.

Men can encourage constructive and inclusive versions of masculinity that place a premium on empathy, teamwork, and emotional expression. This entails resisting toxic masculinity and the urge to live up to negative masculinity norms.

Being Role Models

By exemplifying what it means to be respectful, egalitarian, and supportive partners and allies through their behaviors and attitudes, men can act as great role models for younger generations.

Men can engage in continual learning about issues related to gender equality, realizing that it is a process that is ongoing. It is crucial to reflect on oneself and be willing to unlearn damaging thoughts and actions.

Men may promote diversity and inclusion initiatives at work by arguing for equal pay, varied hiring procedures, and the treatment of all employees equally, regardless of gender.

In the end, men have a crucial part to play in building a more just and equal society where everyone has the chance to flourish and live without prejudice. Men's active participation in the effort to achieve gender equality is crucial for advancement because it is a common objective that benefits everyone.

Chapter 6

Engaging in Constructive Dialogue

For a number of reasons, constructive discussion between feminists and their detractors is crucial.

Increasing Understanding

Through dialogue, feminists and their detractors can better comprehend one another's viewpoints. It gives the chance to dispel misconceptions, rectify false assumptions, and grasp the subtleties of many points of view.

Refining Arguments

Feminists are forced to evaluate their own arguments and stances when they interact with detractors. It pushes them to improve their advocacy and messaging tactics, which results in better, more convincing justifications.

Perspective-Broadening

Engaging in constructive discourse exposes both feminists and their detractors to a variety of points of view and first-hand experiences. Their viewpoints may be widened as a result of this exposure, resulting in more inclusive and comprehensive discussions of gender issues.

Fostering Empathy

Having a conversation allows people to see the human faces behind opposing perspectives, which fosters empathy. It gives the "other side" a face, which can help people approach debates with greater empathy and compassion.

Finding Common Ground

Having a constructive conversation can frequently reveal points of agreement or common objectives that are not immediately evident. Finding points of agreement can act as a springboard for cooperation and coordination.

For the purpose of settling disputes and addressing complaints, dialogue is a crucial instrument. It gives the parties a place to voice their complaints, discuss alternatives, and try to come to an amicable agreement.

Dialogue is a useful teaching tool for both feminists and their detractors. It gives people the chance to share knowledge, learn from one another, and acquire an understanding of the complexity of gender-related issues.

Influence and Persuasion

Effective communication may persuade. They are more willing to consider and possibly adopt feminist arguments and viewpoints when critics converse respectfully with feminists.

Open and inclusive discussion democratizes the conversation on gender issues. It guarantees that a variety of voices, including those opposed to feminism, are heard and have the chance to participate in the discussion.

Legitimacy and Credibility

Feminist movements' legitimacy and credibility are improved by respectfully and constructively responding to their criticisms. It exhibits a dedication to free speech and a readiness to interact with different viewpoints.

Positive development and progress can be sparked through constructive conversation. It can result in changes to societal norms, public opinion changes, and legislative reforms—all of which are essential for furthering gender equality.

Personal Development

Discussions can help people develop their self-awareness and evolve as people. It fosters intellectual and emotional development by putting people under pressure to consider their own prejudices, ideas, and assumptions.

In conclusion, frank discussion between feminists and those who disagree with them promotes growth, understanding, and constructive change. Any social movement will inevitably experience disagreements and criticism, but how these conflicts are handled will decide whether they cause division or advance efforts to achieve social justice and gender equality.

How to recognize how feminism changes and adapts throughout time, just like any other social movement:

For a complex understanding of feminism's dynamics and influence, it is crucial to acknowledge that it, like every social movement, changes and evolves over time. Here are some important ways to recognize and comprehend the development of feminism:

Study Feminist History

It's crucial to research feminism's past in order to comprehend how it has developed. Recognize that there have been several waves of feminism, each with its own concerns and interests. For instance, the first wave emphasized women's suffrage, the second wave emphasized more legal and societal equality and the third wave concentrated on topics like intersectionality and reproductive rights.

Determine Changing Priorities

Feminism changes as society issues and standards do. For instance, modern feminism emphasizes additional topics like gender identity, climate change, and how technology affects gender equality. Recognize that these shifting priorities are a normal reaction to changing conditions.

Think about Global Perspectives

Feminism is a global movement with a variety of perspectives, not just one. Different areas and cultures may place more emphasis on particular aspects of gender equality and use various tactics. Recognize that feminism takes on several guises to address regional circumstances and issues.

It is important to understand how gender overlaps with other facets of identity, including race, class, sexual orientation, and disability. According to this viewpoint, feminism must change to address these specific intersections because not all women experience gender discrimination in the same manner.

Generational Shifts

There may be changes in feminist priorities and strategies as a result of generational disparities. Younger generations frequently bring to the movement fresh viewpoints and strategies that may be different from those of older generations. Recognize that the movement's vitality is a result of this generational growth.

Include Diverse Voices

Recognize that feminism encompasses a variety of voices and viewpoints. It's not just one philosophy, but rather a wide range of concepts and tactics. Even if their opinions conflict with your own, pay attention to other feminist perspectives and learn from them.

Learn from Criticism

Feminist criticism can offer important insights regarding the movement's development. While some criticisms might not be valid, others might point out areas where feminism has to change and advance. Engage in constructive criticism to promote development and transformation.

Engage with feminist movements and organizations to learn about their present objectives and approaches. Participate in gatherings, workshops, and discussions to learn more about the movement's shifting priorities.

Be Responsive to Change

Accept that one's own beliefs and attitudes may change throughout time. Be willing to reexamine and modify your personal beliefs as you develop.

Support the Evolution

Take an active role in campaigns to improve gender equality to support the continued evolution of feminism. To keep the movement flexible and receptive to changing demands, promote dialogue, inclusivity, and intersectionality.

In conclusion, feminism's continued relevance and efficacy depend on our ability to see how it changes and adapts. Recognize that feminism is dynamic and that progress and change are essential to reaching the goal of gender equality.

Conclusion

The Intricate Scene

For feminism to be understood in a more inclusive and complex way, it is essential to acknowledge the movement's diversity of viewpoints and its many facets. These actions will assist you in doing that:

Start by educating yourself about the history of feminism, including all of its waves, ideas, and influential people. Feminism's multidimensional nature will make sense in the light of its history and development.

Read broadly

Read works from feminists with a variety of experiences, backgrounds, and viewpoints. Feminist authors, academics, activists, and bloggers all fall under this category. Look for resources that discuss feminism from a liberal perspective to intersectional feminism and beyond.

Actively listen to women and gender-nonconforming people who consider themselves feminists. Participate in debates, seminars, and other activities that give you the chance to hear other people's perspectives and experiences.

Recognize how feminism links with other social justice movements like those for environmental justice, LGBTQ+ rights, and people with disabilities. Recognize the connections between these movements and how they contribute to feminism's complexity.

Avoid making assumptions or generalizations about feminists when challenging stereotypes. Recognize that feminism is a varied range of viewpoints rather than a single, unified philosophy. Dispel any preconceived notions you may have about feminists or feminism.

Recognize the significance of intersectionality within feminism and embrace it. As a result of their color, class, sexual orientation, disability, and other intersecting identities, people experience gender inequality in different ways. The importance of addressing these intricate intersections is emphasized by intersectional feminism.

Constructive Dialogue

Have courteous, frank discussions with feminists who have different perspectives. Even if you don't agree on every point, having a constructive conversation can help you comprehend different points of view and discover points in which you do.

Encourage diversity within feminist places and organizations by supporting it. Promote the inclusion of minority viewpoints and voices, and endeavor to establish settings where everyone is treated with respect and heard.

Recognize Changing Priorities

Be aware that feminism changes as a result of shifting societal norms and problems. The movement's priorities may change, and fresh problems can emerge. Be willing to modify your conception of feminism as necessary.

Activists should actively raise the voices of marginalized feminists, particularly those whose viewpoints are frequently overlooked. If you have a platform, use it to share their thoughts and stories.

Don't Think of Feminism as a Monolith

Don't think of feminism as a monolith with a single set of beliefs. Instead, understand that feminism comprises a variety of philosophies and tactics, including ecofeminism, womanism, radical feminism, and more.

Self-education and Reflection

Constantly examine your own biases and beliefs. Encourage yourself to expand and study more about feminism and gender equality.

A Request for Co-operation

It is a worthwhile undertaking to encourage readers to engage with feminism critically and contribute to continuing conversations about social justice and gender equality. The following are some methods to encourage critical engagement:

Making feminist literature, articles, and tools available to your readers will help. Give suggestions for beginning books, videos, podcasts, online courses, and other media that give a basic understanding of feminism and gender issues.

Encourage inclusivity by making a friendly and inclusive atmosphere for conversation. Encourage readers to engage in discussions on feminism from a variety of backgrounds and viewpoints. Make careful you respect and amplify the voices of the marginalized.

Encourage readers to engage in critical thought regarding feminist concepts and ideas. Encourage people to think critically, analyze all available information, and cast doubt on their presumptions. Offer discussion starters or questions that encourage critical reflection.

Highlight Intersectionality

Make sure to emphasize how crucial it is to feminism. Explain to readers how gender interacts with various facets of identity (such as race, class, sexual orientation, and disability) to shape people's experiences and viewpoints.

Introduce readers to the range of feminist perspectives by exploring various feminist viewpoints. Discuss various feminism movements, including radical feminism, womanism, queer feminism, and liberal feminism. Encourage readers to research the variations and similarities between these strategies.

Encourage discourse by establishing settings that are respectful and open. Encourage readers to participate in debates, both online and off, where they may exchange ideas, pose questions, and pick the brains of others. Stress the importance of listening in addition to speaking.

Focus on Current Issues

Discuss current problems and obstacles relating to gender equality. Relate feminism to the news, social movements, and political discussions. Encourage readers to research how feminism might help find solutions to current problems.

Share Personal Testimonies

Share the testimonies and personal accounts of people who have been affected by gender inequality. These stories can humanize feminist problems and increase readers' sense of connection to them.

Encourage media literacy by teaching readers to evaluate how gender and feminism are portrayed in the media. Encourage students to dissect prejudices and stereotypes in media such as movies, advertisements, and news reports.

Provide Useful Resources Give readers information about resources and ways to support gender equality through action. Share groups that are addressing gender-based inequalities through campaigns, projects, and organizations.

Encourage readers to exercise empathy by paying attention to other people's perspectives, especially those of people from various backgrounds. Help them comprehend the role that empathy may play in promoting understanding and societal change.

Celebrate Success

Draw attention to examples of advancement and beneficial change in the area of gender equality. Recognize the accomplishments of feminist movements and those who have helped society change for the better.

Establish a Safe Environment

Make sure your website or online community is a respected, safe place where readers may share their opinions without being afraid of being harassed or discriminated against.

Lead by Example

As a facilitator of feminism-related discussions, provide an example of courteous dialogue and tolerance for opposing ideas. Demonstrate that it is possible to have difficult conversations while remaining polite.

Encourage Continuous Learning

Remind readers that feminism and gender equality are topics that they should continue to study. Encourage them to keep reading, listening, and participating in the ongoing conversation about these issues.

By using these techniques, you may encourage readers to think critically, expand their knowledge of feminism, and actively participate in conversations about social justice and gender equality.

Please be aware that the purpose of this book summary is to explore feminism's critics and detractors from a variety of angles. It is crucial to address this topic sensitively and with the knowledge that feminism covers a wide range of viewpoints and objectives and that not all criticisms are applicable to the entire movement.